Horses

Printed and bound in Great Britain by
Hazell Watson & Viney Ltd, Aylesbury
for the Publishers, W. H. Allen & Co. Ltd,
44 Hill Street, London W1X 8LB

ISBN 0 491 02655 2

Horses

Edited by
Elizabeth Rudd

W. H. Allen · London
A Howard & Wyndham Company
1981

Hast thou given the horse strength?
Hast thou clothed his neck in thunder?
The glory of his nostrils is terrible.
He paweth in the valley and rejoiceth
    in his strength.
He goeth on to meet the armed men.
He mocketh at fear and is not affrighted,
Neither turneth he back from the sword
The quiver rattleth against him.
The glittering spear and the shield.
He swalloweth the ground with fierceness
    and rage.

THE BOOK OF JOB

The wise horse cares not
How fast a man may run.

ARMENIAN PROVERB

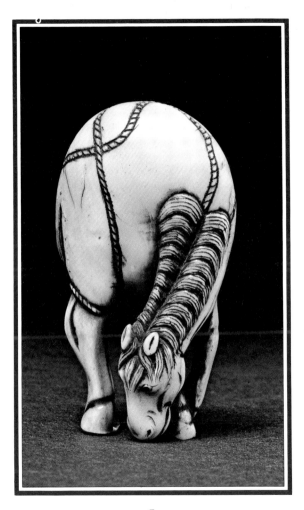

I will not change my horse with any that treads but on four pasterns. Ça, ha! He bounds from the earth, as if his entrails were hairs: le cheval volant, the Pegasus, qui a les narines de feu! When I bestride him, I soar, I am a hawk: he trots the air; the earth sings when he touches it; the basest horn of his hoof is more musical than the pipe of Hermes.

WILLIAM SHAKESPEARE
HENRY V

'Is my team ploughing,
    That I was used to drive
And hear the harness jingle
    When I was man alive?'

Ay, the horses trample,
    The harness jingles now;
No change though you lie under
    The land you used to plough.

A. E. HOUSMAN
A SHROPSHIRE LAD

Alexander had a hoss
Which he called Bucephalus.

ETONIAN PUNTING DITTY

13

When a man is once well run away with, the first thing that occurs to him, I imagine, is how to stop his horse; but men by no means agree in their modes of bringing this matter about. Some will run him at a ditch; which I allow to be a promising experiment if he leaps ill, or not at all. Frenchmen, (and the French are excellent horsemen) will ride against one another; no bad way either: and I have seen riders make directly for a stable (if a door happens to be open) with good effect . . .

GEOFFREY GAMBADO
AN ACADEMY FOR GROWN HORSEMEN

15

There is no secret so close as that between a rider and his horse.

ROBERT SMITH SURTEES
MR SPONGE'S SPORTING TOUR

A monk there was, a fair for the mastery;
An out-ridér that lovèd venerie;
Greyhounds he had, as swift as fowl in flight.
A manly man, to be an abbot able.
Full many a dainty horse had he in stable;
And when he rode, men might his bridle hear
Gingle in a whistling wind so clear,
And eke as loud, as doth the chapel bell.

GEOFFREY CHAUCER
THE MONK 1380

CHAUCER.

(FROM THE ELLESMERE MS.)

A horse that has once won a prize at Newmarket, immediately becomes famous over all England: his name is to be seen in all the papers, and is quickly as well known as that of the best writer in his age; his picture is engraved, and all the country gentlemen adorn their parlours with it. I do not say this to the discredit of the engraver, who finds his end in what he does; but to the shame of the customer: for a print of this kind will sell better than a portrait of Sir Isaac Newton.

LE BLANC
LETTERS FROM ENGLAND

Oh wasn't it naughty of Smudges?
   Oh, Mummy, I'm sick with disgust.
She threw me in front of the Judges,
   And my silly old collarbone's bust.

JOHN BETJEMAN
HUNTER TRIALS

Ride a cock-horse to Banbury Cross,
    To see a fine lady ride on a white horse!
Rings on her fingers and bells on her toes,
    She shall have music wherever she goes.

NURSERY RHYME

Every one knows that horse-racing is carried on mainly for the delight and profit of fools, ruffians, and thieves.

GEORGE GISSING
THE PRIVATE PAPERS OF HENRY RYECROFT

To prevent his favourite horse Incitatus from growing restive, Caligula always picketed the grounds with troops on the day before the races, ordering them to maintain absolute silence. Incitatus owned a marble stable, an ivory stall, purple blankets and a jewelled collar; also a house, furniture, and slaves – to provide suitable entertainment for guests invited in its name. He even planned to award Incitatus a consulship, it is said.

SUETONIUS
THE TWELVE CAESARS

Now a polo-pony is like a poet. If he is born with a love for the game he can be made. The Maltese Cat knew that bamboos grew solely in order that polo-balls might be turned from their roots, that grain was given to ponies to keep them in hard condition, and that ponies were shod to prevent them slipping on a turn. But, besides, all these things, he knew every trick and device of the finest game of the world, and for two seasons he had been teaching the others all he knew or guessed.

RUDYARD KIPLING
THE MALTESE CAT

Her neck is light and well arched, the wither high, the shoulder well sloped, and the quarters so fine and powerful that it is impossible she should be otherwise than a very fast mare. Her length of limb above the hock is remarkable, as is that of the pastern. She carries her tail high, as all well-bred Arabians do, and there is a neatness and finish about every movement, which remind one of a fawn or a gazelle. We are all agreed that she is incomparably superior to anything we have seen here or elsewhere, and would be worth a king's ransom, if kings were still worth ransoming.

LADY ANNE BLUNT
THE BLUNTS IN SYRIA

Five hundred tons of paper
Three miles of broken glass
And what with bags
And packets of fags
You cannot see the grass

ANON
DERBY DAY

'The great art of riding,' the Knight suddenly began in a loud voice, waving his right arm as he spoke, 'is to keep——' Here the sentence ended as suddenly as it had begun, as the Knight fell heavily on top of his head exactly in the path where Alice was walking. She was quite frightened this time, and said in an anxious tone, as she picked him up, 'I hope no bones are broken?'

'None to speak of,' the Knight said, as if he didn't mind breaking two or three of them. 'The great art of riding, as I was saying, is – to keep your balance properly. Like this, you know——' He let go the bridle, and stretched out both his arms to show Alice what he meant, and this time he fell flat on his back, right under the horse's feet.

'Plenty of practice!' he went on repeating, all the time that Alice was getting him on his feet again.

LEWIS CARROLL
ALICE THROUGH THE LOOKING GLASS

He wheels his horse with a touch
Sword in hand. How Exquisite.

YOSHIMOTO

39

The horses of Achilles stood apart from the battle weeping, since they had learnt that their charioteer had fallen in the dust beneath the hands of man-slaying Hector. Automedon whipped them with his swift lash, cajoled them with gentle words, and threatened them, but the pair would neither return to the ships on the Hellespont, nor go back into the battle. They remained immoveable before their beautiful chariot, bowing their heads to the earth. Hot tears flowed from their eyes as they mourned in sorrow for their charioteer, and their long manes were soiled as they streamed down from the yoke cushion. When Zeus saw their grief he took pity on them. 'Poor creatures! Why did I give you to King Peleus who is a mortal destined for death; You who are immortal. What have you to do with man, who of all beasts on the earth is the most miserable?'

HOMER
THE ILIAD

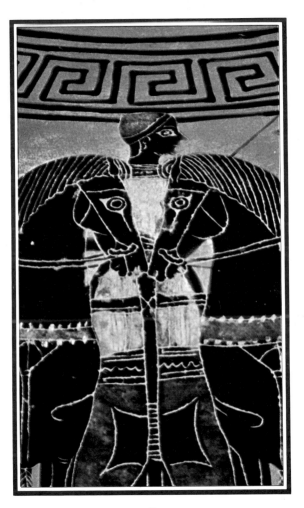

The King of France's horses
are better housed than I.

ERNST AUGUST
ELECTOR OF HANOVER

Women who ride, as a rule, ride better than men. They, the women, have always been instructed; whereas men have usually come to ride without any instruction. They are put upon ponies when they are all boys, and put themselves upon their fathers' horses as they become hobbledehoys: and thus they obtain power of sticking on to the animal while he gallops and jumps, – and even while he kicks and shies: and, so progressing, they achieve an amount of horsemanship which answers the purposes of life. But they do not acquire the art of riding with exactness, as women do, and rarely have such hands as a woman has on a horse's mouth. The consequence of this is that women fall less often than men, and the field is not often thrown into the horror which would arise were a lady known to be in a ditch with a horse lying on her.

ANTHONY TROLLOPE
THE LADY WHO RIDES TO HOUNDS

With a heart of furious fancies
Whereof I am commander,
With a burning spear,
And a horse of air,
To the wilderness I wander.

ANON
TOM O'BEDLAM

'Unting is all tha's worth living for – all time is lost wot is not spent in 'unting – it is like the hair we breathe – if we have it not we die – it's the sport of kings, the image of war without its guilt, and only twenty-five per cent of its danger.

ROBERT SMITH SURTEES
HANDLEY CROSS

The best thing for the inside of a man
is the outside of a horse.

LORD PALMERSTON

And Allah created of the handful of wind a horse of a chestnut colour, like gold, and said to the horse: Behold I have created thee and made thee Arabian, and thou shalt have station and power above all things of the beasts that are subject to man. And I have bound all fortune and treasure to thy loins and on thy back a rich spoil, and to thy forelock a fair issue. And Allah set loose the swift runner and he went on his way neighing.

BEDOUIN LEGEND

Illustration acknowledgements

For permission to use copyright material we are indebted to the following:

Macmillan & Co., Ltd, for an extract from *The Maltese Cat* by Rudyard Kipling; John Murray Ltd, for an extract from 'Hunter Trials' by John Betjeman, from *Collected Poems*; George Harrap & Co., Ltd, for an extract from *A Shropshire Lad* by A. E. Housman.